Savvy Saving

Cavendish
Square
New York

Carolyn E. W. Spath

Published in 2015 by Cavendish Square Publishing, LLC
243 5th Avenue, Suite 136, New York, NY 10016

First Edition

Website: cavendishsq.com

CPSIA Compliance Information: Batch #WW15CSQ

All websites were available and accurate when this book was sent to press.

Library of Congress Cataloging-in-Publication Data

Spath, Carolyn E. W.
Savvy saving / Carolyn E. W. Spath.
pages cm. — (First-glance finance)
Includes index.
ISBN 978-1-50260-096-7 (hardcover) ISBN 978-1-50260-101-8 (ebook)
1. Savings accounts—Juvenile literature. 2. Saving and investment—Juvenile literature. 3. Finance—Juvenile
literature. I. Title.

HG1660.A3S63 2015
332.024—dc23

2014015962

Editor: Amy Hayes
Senior Copy Editor: Wendy A. Reynolds
Art Director: Jeffrey Talbot
Senior Designer: Amy Greenan
Senior Production Manager: Jennifer Ryder-Talbot
Production Editor: David McNamara
Photo Research by J8 Media

The photographs in this book are used by permission and through the courtesy of: Cover photos by Rich
Legg/E+/Getty Images, Juan Camilo Bernal/Moment Open/Getty Images; Rich Legg/E+/Getty Images, 1;
lendy16/Shutterstock.com, throughout; © iStockphoto.com/percds, 5; Iakov Filimonov/Shutterstock.com, 7;
© B Christopher/Alamy, 8; absolute-india/Shutterstock.com, 11; Klaus Tiedge/Blend Images/Getty Images,
13; gstockstudio/Shutterstock.com, 15; Purestock/Getty Images, 17; Dioma/Textures: Paper/deviantART,
18; Dioma/Textures: Paper/deviantART, 20; George Doyle/Stockbyte/Getty Images, 25; jamie cross/
Shutterstock.com, 26; JGI/Jamie Grill/Blend Images/Getty Images, 27; © iStockphoto.com/robynmac, 30;
Neil Overy/Photolibrary/Getty Images, 32; Keith Brofsky/Stockbyte/Getty Images, 36; Richard Cano/E+/
Getty Images, 38; © iStockphoto.com/csdesigns, 39; Margaret M Stewart/Shutterstock.com, 40; JGI/Jamie
Grill/Blend Images/Getty Images, 41.

Printed in the United States of America

CONTENTS

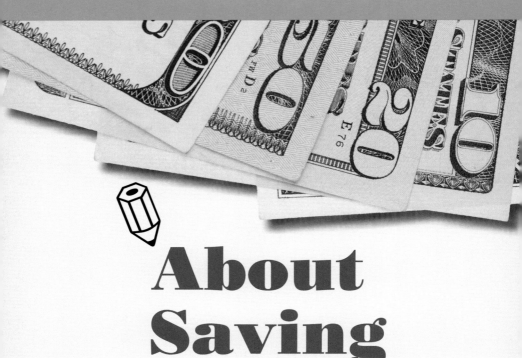

CHAPTER ONE

About Saving

S aving is an important part of all aspects of our lives. When we save, we keep something we have right now so that we can use it in the future. Saving and planning for the future can be applied to many things, including the food we eat. Today, your family may buy food at the grocery store, but this was not always possible. Before grocery stores, most families had to grow their own food. These families would grow all the food that they could during the warm months. Instead of eating it all at once, they would only eat some

Saving part of their harvest for winter use is one way that early people practiced saving.

of what had been grown. The rest of the food they grew was saved for future use. Throughout the winter when food was harder to find, families would eat the food that they had stored during the warmer months. This is one way that early people learned to save. Now that grocery stores are common, fresh food is available to most people all year long. This means that far fewer people need to save food for the winter. While they may not need to save food in the same way, people have learned to save other things.

Saving For All Sorts of Things

Do you ever save things for later? Maybe you save the last of your Halloween candy each year. If you make jewelry, you might save your favorite beads. If you like to draw, you might save some crayons in your favorite colors. People save all sorts of things. From stamps to old cars to spare change, people love to save.

Although people save different things, the reasons that people save are generally the same. People save things that they like or value. They save things that are

Early Money

In early civilizations people would barter, or trade, with one another to obtain the things they needed. The Ancient Egyptians were the first to invent money to use instead of bartering. Around 2500 BCE the Egyptians started to exchange small metal discs for goods or services that they needed instead of bartering. These small discs were the first coins and the first money as we think of it today.

Saving jewelry is very common. It can be worn again or taken apart and recycled to make something new.

difficult to get now, or may become difficult to find in the future. Think of the family saving food for the winter. The food is valuable because it allows the family to eat. It needed to be saved because it would be far more difficult for them to obtain during the winter.

The Greenback

During the American Civil War, the U.S. government needed money that was easy to produce and use in order to help fund the war. As a result, the United States Treasury printed the first paper money in the United States on July 17, 1861. These early bills were called "greenbacks" because of their color.

One common thing that adults have to save is money. Adults go to work so that they have money. They save money because it allows them to buy the things that they want and need, and because money can be hard to get. With money, adults are able to buy groceries, clothes, and everything else their families needs. By saving some of their money they are making sure that they will be able to buy the things that their families will need in the future.

A Penny Saved...

How do you get money? Most kids don't have professional jobs yet, but many earn money from their parents for doing chores around the house or for doing small jobs for a neighbor or family member. Perhaps you have received money as a gift during special events, such as your birthday or a holiday. It is likely that you spend your money in a different way than adults. You might buy things that are fun, but not have to worry about things you need. For instance, instead of groceries you buy candy bars, or instead of a house you might save up to buy a phone or a game. However, just like it is for adults, it is difficult for you to earn money, and you want to use it to get things that are important to you. In this book, you will learn about different ways to protect the money you have, use your money more effectively, and save up for something you want.

CHAPTER TWO

Why Save?

· ·

Saving money is the practice of setting some **funds** aside to spend in the future. It can be as simple as adding spare change to your piggy bank each week. The important thing is to have some money set aside so that you can pay for your **expenses**, or the things you buy.

Let's say you know you are going to your favorite bookstore next week. You know you want to buy the newest installment of your favorite series, but it costs two dollars more than your weekly allowance. You decide to keep two dollars of your allowance from this week to add to next week's allowance. By doing this, you'll have enough money for the book when you get to the store. That is saving for a **short-term expense**.

It is important to save money so that you are better prepared to handle future expenses, even if you only save a few coins.

Short-term expenses are anything that you expect to buy in the next few months, such as a video game or movie that is coming out soon.

Planning Ahead

When you save for something that is a year or more away, it is called a **long-term expense**. Long-term expenses are usually more expensive items, such as saving for college or your first car. For short-term expenses it is easy to save your money in a jar or other safe place, but for bigger, long-term expenses it is a good idea to work with a bank or other financial institution to open a **savings account**. By using a savings account, the bank keeps your money safe while your savings grow.

Look at the expense table below. Can you tell if they are long-term or short-term expenses? What are some other examples from your own life?

Expense	Time Frame	Short-term	Long-term
College	10 years		X
Video Game	1 month	X	
First Car	8 years		X
Lego™ Set	1 month	X	

Saving money is not just for kids. As you get older it becomes even more important to save for the future. A common savings goal among adults is to save for **retirement**. When you get too old to work, your retirement savings are used to cover all of your expenses. These expenses will include everything from necessities such as food and housing to fun things such as going on a trip or going to a show. People save for retirement in many ways. Some adults work with banks directly to save for retirement using individual retirement accounts, or IRAs. Other adults may work for companies that contribute to their retirement savings through a pension plan or 401(k) plan. As you grow up and start working, it is important to start saving for retirement as soon as you can.

This couple planned carefully for retirement so that they would be able to travel when they stopped working.

Rainy Day Savings

Sometimes it is impossible to know that a large expense is coming until it arrives. That is why it is important to save some money for an emergency fund. Rainy Day Savings is a just-in-case fund, just in case the roof leaks on a rainy day, for example. Think of this type of savings as having money just in case something happens. For adults, it might be just in case they get sick or can't work. Having three months of expenses set aside can help pay for food, bills, and other necessary expenses while they get on their feet again. Your "just in case" is probably different now than it will be when you are older. What sort of emergency might you need to plan for? You might

Saving for College

What do you plan to be when you grow up? You could be a mechanic, a police officer, a teacher, or any number of professions. Whatever you choose, you will probably need some specialized training after high school either at a college or vocational school. This important step in your education can be very expensive. Yearly tuition at a state college can be over $8,500 per year. By saving for college today, you can make it easier to achieve your dreams in the future. Here are some ways that you and your parents can get started:

1. Research what kind of education you need for several types of jobs that appeal to you.

2. Start a dedicated college savings account like an Educational Savings Account.

3. Commit to make regular **deposits** into your college savings account.

College is a great experience, but it can be very expensive.
Saving for college early will make it easier to afford.

break the chain on your bicycle, or tear your backpack.
Emergency expenses can be different for everyone, and
it is hard to know what they might be until one happens.
By setting money aside for an emergency now, you can
be protected if one does arrive.

Learning to save money while you are young can help
you establish good financial habits for the rest of your
life. By setting clear savings goals you can anticipate your
expenses and plan ahead for them, whether they are
short-term expenses, like a new Lego™ set, or long-
term expenses, like college.

CHAPTER THREE

Managing Money

. . . .

Planning to Save

The best way to save money is the way that works for you. Whether you save in a piggy bank or a bank account, it is important to have a plan. Your plan should be clear and easy to follow so that it becomes part of your routine. Whether you are saving for a new computer or a college fund, the basic parts of your plan should be the same.

Set a Goal

To understand these steps better, let's use Mia as an example. Mia is in fifth grade and wants to save her

By making a realistic plan, and sticking to it, Mia was able to buy the new bicycle she needed.

birthday money toward something big. Her first step is to make a list of items she wants. You can follow along by making your own list.

Mia realizes that she cannot have everything on her list. She narrows the list down by first eliminating items that do not make sense. For instance, Mia cannot have a dog because her mother is allergic to dogs. Also, there is no room for a swimming pool in her apartment building. She crosses them both out on her list. Next, she numbers the remaining

Checklist
1. Set a goal
2. Know your money
3. Pay yourself

items based on what she needs most. For Mia, a bicycle is most important because she will need a bike to get to middle school next year.

Are there items on your list that do not make sense? Cross those items out first. Then rank what is most important to you. If you have trouble deciding, try asking yourself, "Why it is worth saving my money?"

Mia's Wish List
Bicycle - 1
Computer - 2
Camera - 3
~~Dog~~
~~Swimming Pool~~

Now that Mia knows what she is saving for, she needs to know how much a new bike will cost. She and her mother do some research online and talk to a salesman at a local bicycle shop. From this research, Mia knows she can get the bicycle she wants for $250. It's a lot of money, but her parents agree that if Mia saves her money they will split the cost with her.

Mia's savings goal is half of the $250 needed for a new bicycle, $250 ÷ 2 = $125 or:

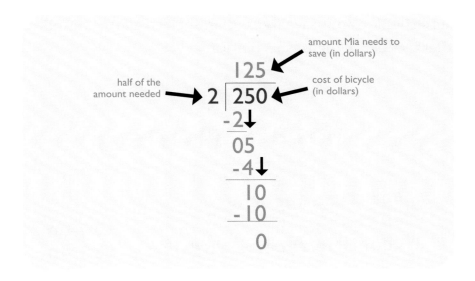

Know Your Money

Now that Mia has a goal, she needs to figure out how she is going to reach it. In order to do that she needs to understand her expected **income**. That is how much she expects to receive. To do this, she lists out all of her sources of income in two categories. The first category is for money Mia receives only once a year. Mia has $35.00 remaining from her recent birthday. Her birthday only happens once a year. Every week Mia receives $5.00 in allowance for doing the dishes and $10.00 each week for walking her neighbor's dogs.

From this Mia knows that she has $35.00 and can expect to earn $15.00 each week. If Mia were to try to save all $15.00 each week she would not be able to pay for things she needs such as snacks at her after school program or dues for her scout troop. In order to make sure she does not save more than she can afford, Mia adds these weekly expenses to her list.

Mia's Money

One-Time Income

Birthday	$35.00
One-time Income Total =	$35.00

Weekly Income

Allowance	$5.00
Dog Walking	$10.00
Weekly Income Total =	$15.00

Weekly Expenses

Snack	$8.00
Scouts	$2.00
Weekly Expenses Total =	$10.00

How Can You Earn More?

As you look closely at your money you may realize that meeting your savings goal will be harder than expected. One thing you can do to reach your goal faster is to look for ways to earn money. Talk to your parents about ways you can earn. They may suggest chores you could do to earn extra money, or help you set up a lemonade stand.

When you subtract Mia's weekly expenses from her weekly income,

Income	$15
- Expenses	$10
Difference	$5

you see that Mia has $5 per week remaining.

From this $5.00 per week, Mia will have to save for her bicycle and buy everything else that she needs over the next few months. With this in mind she decides she can afford to save $3 each week. This will leave Mia $2 each week in case of unexpected expenses.

To find out how long it will take Mia to reach her savings goal, she will have to find out how much is left to be saved and divide that number by the amount she is saving each week.

Savings Goal   **$125**
- Current Savings   **$35**

Amount to be Saved   **$90**

Amount to be Saved ÷ Weekly Savings = Number of Weeks to Reach Goal

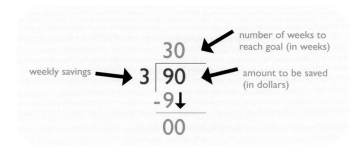

Mia's savings plan is to save $3 per week for 30 weeks until she reaches her goal of $125 for her new bicycle. What is your savings plan?

Treasure between the
Couch Cushions

Do you ever find pennies in your pockets or in between the couch cushions? Make a point of adding this spare change to your savings. You will not notice a few extra pennies missing from your spending money, but you will be amazed at how quickly they add up when you put them all together.

Pay Yourself First

When you save money today, you make that money available for you to use weeks or months in the future. In this way savings is a way of paying yourself. There is an old saying in savings that goes, "Pay yourself first." This means that you should put money into your savings before you pay for other things. It comes from the idea that it is easier to save money when you are not carrying it in your pocket with your spending money. For Mia, this means that she should put her $3 in savings each week as soon as she gets paid.

As you get started with your savings plan you might forget to pay yourself. If some weeks you cannot save as much as you wanted to, do not be discouraged. Everyone misses a week every now and then. Just save what you can and go back to following your plan the next week.

CHAPTER FOUR

Fighting Temptation

Opportunity Costs

For many people trying to save money, the first few months can be the hardest part. You might be tempted to take money from your savings to buy other things that you think you want, such as a movie ticket or a candy bar. The things you would buy if you were not saving your money are called **opportunity costs**. For example, you may face the choice between spending $2 on a candy bar and putting the same $2 into your savings. If you decide to save the $2, the candy bar would be your opportunity cost. What opportunity costs are you giving up by saving your money?

24   **Savvy Saving**

It can be hard to say "no" to jellybeans. When you are tempted to spend your savings, think about the items for which you are saving.

At some point you may think that the opportunity cost is too high, and be tempted to take money out of your savings for little things such as an extra candy bar or a new toy. By thinking about these things in advance, you can be better prepared when temptation strikes. Now that you have thought of all of the things you will be giving up by saving your money, think about your savings goal and why it is important to you. If you are saving for a new bicycle, like Mia, where will you ride it? If you are saving for college, what will you study when you get there? Whatever you are saving for, think about how much happier it will make you in the long run than that extra candy bar will now.

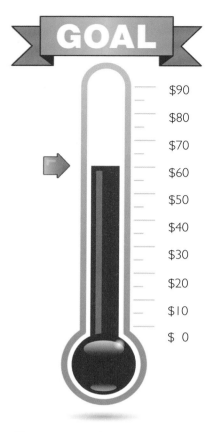

GOAL

$90
$80
$70
$60
$50
$40
$30
$20
$10
$ 0

Charts are a fun way to track your saving.

Making It Easier

Even with your goal in mind opportunity costs can be hard to resist. There are some things you can do to make it easier. The first thing you can do is to make sure you are not trying to save more than you can afford. It is important to keep some **spending money** available so that you can buy some of the other things you want, just like Mia did in the last chapter. If you do not, saving will be too hard and you will be less likely to keep saving in the long run.

A good way to make saving easier and more enjoyable is to see how much you've saved. For some people, it helps to keep their savings in a special place. This can be as easy as making a savings jar. Simply find a clear jar or other container with a lid and decorate it with a picture of the item for which you are saving. The picture will remind you of why you are saving and help you stay focused on your goal. Put your savings jar in a safe place where you will see it often, such as your dresser at home. Because the jar is clear, you can watch your savings grow. The lid

Save, Spend, Share

In addition to saving and spending your money, you could also choose to share your money. Kids give to food pantries, medical research, religious groups, and so much more. Talk to your parent or guardian about with whom you could share some of your money.

Once you have an organization in mind, decorate three jars, one for saving, one for spending money, and one for sharing. Every time you get money, put some in each jar. When your sharing jar gets full, donate it to the cause of your choice.

will make you stop and think before taking money out of the jar for other things.

Another way to stay focused is to track your progress. Make a big chart with your savings goal at the top and markings to show how close you are. Hang your chart in a visible location, such as your bedroom door. Each week, as you add money to your jar, color in a portion of the chart until you reach the top. Many professional fundraisers use charts such as these because they really help motivate people to reach their goals.

Good Habits

After a few weeks of saving you may notice that you think about your opportunity costs less often, or these things may seem less important to you. As you get closer to your goal you may even find yourself getting excited about saving. These are all good signs that saving money is becoming a habit for you. After you meet your first savings goal, keep putting money in your savings jar each week. If you start to earn more money, try saving a little bit more. If you do not have a new savings goal right away, that is okay. Saving is always a good idea. You can start your own emergency fund, just in case something unexpected comes up.

Once you have a money-saving habit, it can stay with you for the rest of your life. By developing these skills now, you will be ready to keep saving money as an adult. Then, your savings habit will help you to buy a home, travel the world, or simply be prepared when something unexpected happens.

CHAPTER FIVE

Understanding Banks

....

Bank Accounts

Saving in a jar is a great way to get started, but as you keep saving that jar is going to get pretty full. Banks can help people save by holding on to money in bank accounts. There are many advantages to a bank account.

If you keep your savings at home and you lose it, that money is gone. A bank account can help keep money safe. By national law, banks in the United States guarantee that if anything should happen to the bank, your money will be returned up to $100,000 per account. This means that if the bank is robbed or closes down, you will be able to get your money back.

Another advantage of using a bank is that you get paid for it. When you deposit your money in a bank account, the bank uses that money to **invest** and lend to other people. This is how a bank earns money. In exchange for letting the bank use your money, the bank pays a small percentage of their earnings back to you in the form of **interest**. The amount of interest your money will earn relates to how much money you have in the bank and how long you leave it there. The more you leave in the bank, the more interest you will earn.

If your savings jar is overflowing, it might be time to consider a savings account.

Here is a chart that shows how much money you would have if you saved ten dollars a month in a savings account versus ten dollars a month in a piggy bank. Which way do you save more?

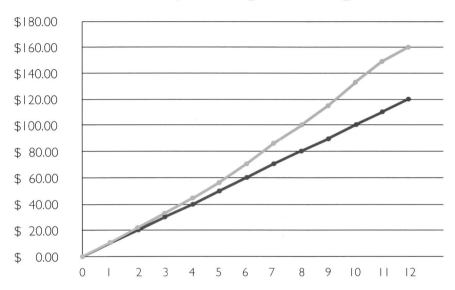

Comparing Savings

Banks offer many different kinds of accounts and other services to help people manage their money effectively. The two main types of bank accounts you should be aware of are **checking accounts** and savings accounts. A checking account is designed to hold money that the account holder wants to be able to access quickly and easily. This type of account may earn little or no interest, but provides access to money without carrying cash. Many young people open their first checking account when

Not All Cards
Are the Same

I t can be easy to confuse a **credit card** with a **debit card**, but the two are not the same. When someone pays with a debit card the money is taken out of their bank account directly, as if they paid cash. With a credit card, the credit company pays for the item and the cardholder agrees to pay that credit company for it later, usually with interest.

they get their first job because these accounts provide an easy way to deposit their paychecks. You may notice your parents using a paper check or debit card to make everyday purchases like paying for bills or groceries.

A savings account is designed to hold more money for a longer period of time than a checking account. This type of account is a great way to start saving toward college or your other long-term savings goals. Savings accounts always earn interest, and may have special rules to encourage people to leave more of their money in the bank. These rules may include limits on the number of times money can be taken out of the account each month, or minimum balance requirements. A balance refers to how much money is in a bank account. Minimum balance requirements describe the least amount of money that can be kept in an account without facing a penalty. It is important to ask your bank about these rules when you open an account.

Investments

In addition to bank accounts, banks also offer a range of products to help customers invest their money. Unlike money in a bank account, it is difficult to access money that has been invested, and there is no guarantee that investors will earn money. Sometimes investors actually lose money. How much an investment can earn is tied to how risky it is.

When investors buy **stock**, they buy a portion of a company because they think that company will succeed.

Comparing Bank Accounts

Sometimes banks have special offers for new customers to encourage them to open accounts. They may give things away or offer special interest rates for the first few months. These special offers might be nice, but they are a bad reason to choose a bank account. Instead, look for an account with a high interest rate and low fees.

If the investor is right and that company does well, that stock pays money called **dividends**. This means that the investor has gained money. However, if the company does poorly, the stock might be worth less than the price the investor paid for it. If this happens, then the investor has lost money. Because stocks can earn or lose value they are considered high-risk investments.

Bonds are a less risky form of investment. When investors buy a bond they lend money to an organization, often the government. In exchange for being able to borrow the money, the organization selling the bonds agrees to pay the investor the price of the bond plus interest. If the organization is unable to pay its bondholders, the money is lost.

CHAPTER SIX

Opening a Savings Account

Choosing the Right Account

Now that you have a better understanding of saving money, you can talk to your parent or guardian about opening a savings account. Like any big decision, the first step is to get your parent's approval. The bank will require your legal guardian to open the savings account with you and share responsibility for the account until you are old enough to manage it on your own. For most banks, this will be when you are eighteen years old.

Opening a bank account is both exciting and confusing. Investigate with your parent so that you both understand what is involved.

Once you and your parent agree to open a savings account, you can work together to research what type of savings account will work best for you. The Internet can be a great place to start your research. Most banks have websites that explain their savings accounts. You can also go to a bank you trust and ask what kinds of services they have available for kids. Here are some things to keep in mind as you do your research:

1. *Location* – If you intend to go to the bank often, it is important to choose one that is conveniently located. It may be easiest for you to go to the same bank as your parent or to use one that is

walking distance from your house. If going to the bank in person is not important to you, you might even consider using an online bank.

2. *Fees and Minimum Balance Requirements* – Sometimes banks charge high fees for small accounts or accounts that are not used very often. If you do not have a lot of money to put in your bank account when you are first setting it up, these fees could cost you more than you save. Be sure to look for a savings account that doesn't have fees for small deposits or minimum balance requirements.

3. *Interest Rates* – Interest is money that a bank pays you for keeping your money in a savings account. Rates are the level of interest paid out over one year called the **annual percent yield,** or APY. The higher the APY on your account, the faster your savings will grow.

4. *Age* – Many banks offer special savings accounts for kids less than eighteen years old. These accounts are designed to help you learn to save. The accounts frequently offer higher interest rates, and lower fees to make it easier for your money to grow.

At the Bank

Once you find the right savings account for you, you and your parent will need to apply for an account. Some banks allow you to open an account online or over the

The bank needs proof that you are who you say you are. That is why you need to bring so many documents with you.

phone, but if you are opening an account in person, you should bring your birth certificate, Social Security card, and something the shows where you live such as a piece of mail that has your name and address on it. If you also have a passport or an identification card with your picture on it, those are also good items to bring.

The banker will help you fill out an application by asking you questions. Take the time to ask questions if you do not understand something about the account, and to read over all of the forms you are given with your parent or guardian. When you leave, keep these forms, as well as your account number, in a safe place.

Making a Deposit

Once your account is set up, you will need to make deposits by putting money into your account using a **deposit slip**. You may receive these when you open your account. If not, they are always available at the bank. You will need to fill out your name, the date you are making the deposit, your account number, and how much money you are depositing. A typical deposit slip is shown below.

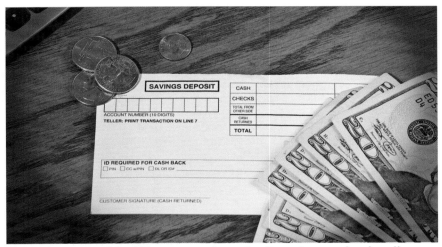

If you have trouble filling out a deposit slip, ask your bank teller to show you how. That way you will be ready next time.

To fill out how much money you are depositing, write the total amount of dollars and change you are putting in the bank next to the line for "Cash." Then, write the value of each check you are depositing on a separate line in the section labeled "Checks." Add up all of your cash and checks to get your "Subtotal." If you want to

Endorsing Checks

Look at the back of a check you have received. There is a small box on the top with an "X" in it. You endorse a check by signing your name next to the X. Your signature, or endorsement, shows the bank that you are the one who received the money from the check. If a check is made out to you but someone else will be putting it in the bank for you, write "For deposit only" instead of signing your name.

deposit only part of a check instead of putting it in the bank, fill out the amount you want to keep in the line for "Less cash." Subtract the line "Less Cash" from the "Subtotal" to find your "Total." Finally, hand your deposit slip, cash, and endorsed checks to the bank teller. The teller will give you a receipt showing how much money you deposited.

Make saving part of your routine by depositing money in your savings jar or bank account on a regular basis.

Whether you save at the bank or at home the most important thing is that you save. Remember the key steps to a good saving plan are to (1) set a clear savings goal, (2) know your money, and (3) pay yourself first by saving as soon as you get paid. By keeping to these steps, you will soon be reaching your goals. Good luck, and savvy saving!

annual percent yield (APY) A yearly return on an investment that must be provided by banks.

bond A certificate that shows that an individual has agreed to lend money to a government or business. In exchange, the borrower has agreed to pay back the money that was borrowed with interest by a specific time.

checking account A bank account which allows you to make charges against your balance using checks or a debit card.

credit card A card that allows the cardholder to receive goods and services now but pay for them with interest in the future. The credit card company pays for the services at the time of purchase, and the cardholder pays the credit card company at a specific date in the future.

debit card A card that allows the cardholder to access funds in their checking account, often for the purchase of goods or services.

deposit Money put into an account.

deposit slip A form used at banks to make it possible to put money into an account.

dividend The amount of money that a stock gains from increasing in value.

expense The amount that is paid for goods or services.

funds Another term for money.

income Money that is earned.

interest Earnings for letting another person or organization use one's money. Bank interest is paid on deposits in exchange for letting the bank use that money.

invest Using current money to make more money, with the understanding that risk is involved.

long-term expense Something you expect to pay for in the years ahead, usually requiring a lot of saving.

opportunity cost What is given up in exchange for a financial decision.

retirement A time when older adults stop working and begin to live off of their investments.

savings account A bank account which takes in deposits, earns interest, and allows money to be taken out.

short-term expense Something you expect to pay for within the next few months, requiring some saving.

spending money Money that you can use immediately, which is not saved.

stock An investment that reflects a share of ownership in a company.

FIND OUT MORE

Books

Harmon, Hollis Page. *Barron's Money Sense For Kids.*
Hauppauge, NY: Barron's Educational Series, Inc.,1999.

Mayr, Diane. *The Everything Kids Money Book.* Holbrook, MA:
Adams Media Corporation, 2000.

Vallaint, Doris. *Personal Finance—Exploring Business and
Economics.* Philadelphia, PA: Chelsea House Publishers, 2001.

Websites

Bankit
www.bankit.com/youth

Bankit is an interactive website that helps kids and parents learn
about finances and making money decisions in the real world.

DFI KidsPage
www.wdfi.org/ymm/kids/default.asp

This website from the Department of Financial Institutions
State of Wisconsin introduces young financiers to the history
of money, as well as teaches them about positive money-
saving behaviors.

U.S. Department of the Treasury Kids Zone Page
www.treasury.gov/about/education/Pages/kids-zone.aspx

This education page is part of the U.S. Department of
Treasury website, and is chock full of interesting and exciting
links for kids to learn more about money, where it comes
from, and how it is regulated.

INDEX

fees, 37
   and minimum balance
     requirements, 37
   high interest rate and low,
     34
funds, 10

income, 19–21
   categories of, 19
Individual Retirement
   Account (IRA), 12
   See also, 401(k);
     retirement
interest, 30, 34
   and checking accounts, 31
   and credit cards, 32
   and savings accounts, 33
   interest rates, 34, 37
   See also, annual
     percentage yield
     (APY)
invest, 30, 33
   See also, bond; interest;
     retirement

long-term expense, 11

opportunity cost, 24–26, 28

paycheck, 33

Rainy Day Savings, 13
retirement, 12, **13**
   See also, 401(k); Individual
   Retirement Account

savings account, 11, 30–31,
   33, 36
   age, 37
   college savings, 14
   Educational Savings
     Account, 14
   fees, 37
   interest rates, 37
   opening, 35
short-term expense,
   10–11, 15
spending money, 26–27
stock, 33–34

Carolyn E.W. Spath is a new author. This is her first book for young readers. When she isn't writing, Carolyn works for the University of Akron in Lakewood, Ohio, and volunteers with a local Girl Scout troop. She also enjoys cooking, traveling, and spending time with her husband, Tim.